T0148982

Shakespearean Variations

Shakespearean Variations

Ralph McInerny

St. Augustine's Press
South Bend, Indiana
2001

Manufactured in the United States of America.

1 2 3 4 5 6 07 06 05 04 03 02 01

Library of Congress Cataloging in Publication Data
McInerny, Ralph M.
     Shakespearean variations / Ralph McInerny.
          p. cm.
     A reworking of Shakespeare's sonnets, using the
     same first line, the last word in each line, and the
     rhyming scheme.
     ISBN 1-890318-90-6 (alk. paper)
     1. Shakespeare, William, 1564–1616 –
     Adaptations. 2. Sonnets, American. 3. Aging –
     Poetry. I. Shakespeare, William, 1564–1616.
     II. Title.
     PS3563.A31166 S48 2000
     811'.54 – dc21

                                        00-010656

∞ *The paper used in this publication meets the minimum requirements of the*
American National Standard for Information Sciences – Permanence of Pa-
per for Printed Materials, ANSI Z39.48-1984.

1

From fairest creatures we desire increase
That being fat they may before they die
Have such *avoirdupois* that at decease
They'll make a greater claim on memory –
Dew-lapped, lids heavy, pouched eyes,
Poly-chinned, their engine full of fuel
And bellied to obscure the land that lies
Unseen beneath their feet. And is it cruel
To wish that they should cease to ornament
The race, become autumnal, forsake the spring,
That they might share our envious discontent,
Who will not be at table so niggarding.
    Ah love, I really do not wish to be
    Resentful of thy thinness but would fatten thee.

When forty winters shall besiege thy brow
And your ripe wheat will like an autumn field
Reveal the cost of always moving ever through the
    Now,
Become what never yet your mirror beheld,
Then you will fill out questionnaires with lies
And feign forgetfulness of half your days,
Memory dimming as will your lovely eyes
As you grow used to much less frequent praise.
Then will you cry, "Oh what's the use?"
Gone the allurements that were lately thine,
You will gladly borrow time's excuse
And learn to bear the figure that then is thine.
    My dear, at forty you'll be far from old,
    Tis later wait the deeper depths of cold.

Look in the glass and tell the face thou viewest
You really would not wish to be another.
There was a time when you were mankind's newest
And that face nuzzled warmly at its mother
But lately issued from the Eden of the womb,
Slapped and bawling, bathed and oiled and dry,
Inconceivably distant from the tomb,
Incessant cause of all but endless laundry.
Now as adolescents will will you
Desire a far more prepossessing prime
And would when looking in your mirror see
The image of one who is the darling of her time?

    To be otherwise, my dear, is not to be;
    Metamorphosis asks too much of thee.

4

Unthrifty loveliness, why dost thou spend
My earnings as if they were a legacy
Till I must borrow if I am still to lend
You more, who think that luxuries are free?
Will you subject our love to such abuse
And always take and almost never give?
Your youthful years are really no excuse.
Our love must die and I must lonely live.
But O the thought of being all alone
So weighs me down that I cannot deceive
Myself that I could live if you were gone,
Or even wish to, were you to leave.
    My money and my heart are both for thee
    Till you and I both in the poorhouse be.

5

Those hours that with gentle work did frame
The countenance that in this square doth dwell
Will though hours still pass remain the same
Nor ever will your face itself excel.
No duchess first or last will hang upon
My wall or ever take your place there.
The sitters sat and having sat are gone,
But portraits stay when subjects are elsewhere,
And pigments last when flesh has nothing left
Of color, and she who sat, when framed in glass,
Now finds herself of beauty quite bereft
While hours inexorably pass and pass and pass.
    It is not just nor is it truly meet
    That you are not your image now, my sweet.

6

Then let the winter's ragged hand deface
The land as summer's sweetened sounds are stilled,
The sap recedes to roots and in this place
Of frigid air all trace of life is killed
While golden leaves are banked in usury.
Once rushing waters, now on loan
To winter, turn to ice as I to thee
Will turn when we in covered warmth are one.
Nature has become still life, an art
Unlike our own; I hibernate with thee
And cling to borrowed spring till snows depart,
As sleeping seed in earth will have posterity.
>   This winter which to outer eyes is far from fair
>   May yield its fruit and deliver up an heir.

Lo, in the orient when the gracious light
Begins to burnish what was dull, the eye
Once more regains with dawn the power of sight
And throws off dreams for nature's majesty.
There rises on that once more lighted hill
The measure of our life from youth to age,
Our days that multiplied and do so still,
While we continue on this pilgrimage.
As engine pulls along the coupled car,
So sun trails hours that added make our day
From Prime to Compline, little hours that are
But stations to count us as we pass their way.

    But love, our hands now join in brightest noon,
    Warming the blood with promise of a son.

Music to hear, why hear'st thou music sadly?
This measured sound is full of joy
Toward which our greedy ears turn gladly
You're wrong to think we play it to annoy.
If only you would heed quantified sounds
And let their undulations teach your ears;
Disordered passion that unchecked confounds,
When tamed by music, no burden is to bear.
The single listening soul finds its other
Better self when lifted by this ordering,
As bawling babe is silenced by its mother
Who while she gently rocks will also sing.

    Though made of many notes, the song is one,
    Than music sweeter solace is there none.

Is it for fear to wet a widow's eye
That you cling tenaciously to life?
Or is determination not to die
Aimed at yourself instead of at your wife?
Do you fear that, mourning, she would weep
Because your dying left her here behind
With only fading memories to keep?
More likely you would soon be out of mind
For grief is but a meager hoard to spend
And in a month she'd have no more of it.
Her sorrow, thanks to time, will have an end
And she will soon forget the reason of it.

    So linger on as by your bed she sits;
      Impatience is the sin that she commits.

For shame deny that thou bear'st love to any
And make our maker seem improvident
Who said that two should love and thus be many.
That man must cease to be is evident
But love can best indifference and hate.
The flesh against our reason will conspire
Lest frigid folks the race might ruinate.
Ah love, relent, be undone by desire
For it is only a fallacy that mind
Is meant to be indifferent to love,
Since mind must know that gone would be our kind
Did we the flesh's furnace disapprove.
    My love, come warm and reasoning to me,
      And then entwined I'll syllogize with thee.

11

As fast as thou shalt wane so fast thou grow'st.
Thus the poet archaically reportest
As he pentametrically bestowest
Order on counted iambs and then convertest
Measured lines to poetry that by increase
Forestalls sound's inevitable decay,
Words made into music never cease
Or like mere noise are wafted soon away.
Ah reader, let us keep his art in store,
Resolve that by our leave it will not perish
But heard again and yet again will only more
Survive that future ears his lines may cherish.
    The precious must be shared and come thereby
    To permanence and thus forget to die.

When I do count the clock that tells the time
I watch the hands that cross its face till night,
And still must cross till day and hour of prime,
All tenses unified as colors are in white.
Nature measures time with falling leaves,
Insomniacs by counting off the herd,
Reapers count their blessings counting sheaves,
An old man counts the gray hairs in his beard.
God could never such a creature make
As would not in its very coming go,
And in receiving life its very life forsake
As rising sun foretells its setting glow.
    Against the teeth of time we've no defense
    Nor will till that day we are carried hence.

O that you were yourself, but love, you are
Becoming other even as you live,
As infant does the child, so must prepare
The child a further self and selves that give
To one another and in the giving cease
Because they are no longer what they were.
Selves collectively increase and one by one decrease,
Each enduring just as much as it can bear.
Life's dark side is found in its decay,
The law of its survival life must uphold
And die in harmony with the death of day,
Telling out its warmth till it is cold.
   It is the native curse of man to know
      That having come he's sure eventually to go.

14

Not from the stars do I my judgment pluck,
Unlearned in even Ptolemaic astronomy,
Nor do I count on any astral luck
To give our love a star-crossed quality.
I heed the sun by which I tell
The time, whether or no my watch I wind.
I can compute sidereal circuits well
And season from the solstice easily find.
But from the clock within the blood derive
A surer sense of passage than from art
Or artifice. My spring will not survive,
But running on to winter will convert.
    By none of the above could I prognosticate
    My chiseled-in-granite final date.

When I consider every thing that grows,
A feat not done by one in just a minute –
Indeed my ignorance of botany shows
If even on the dandelion I comment.
There is in short the chance of much increase
In what I know of things beneath the sky.
Indeed my knowledge can be said to decrease,
Departing as it will from memory.
Ah, would that I could fashion out a story
That would some wondrous objects bring to sight,
Things quite incapable of decay,
Remaining visible even in the night.
    It will come as no surprise to you
    That I can only make of old things new.

16

But wherefore do not you a mightier way
Than that which leads amid the ravages of time,
Among such beauty as contains its own decay
And robs of reason all its latent rhyme?
Recall the happy hours that we have spent
Reading aloud pages of Sigrid Undset,
Where love and more than love and more than flowers
Flourish though fools may call them counterfeit.
Mortal man is anxious to repair
With chisel and brush and with his running pen
The havoc wrought by time upon the fair,
The flawed, the fatal lot of mortal men.
    Life is made deathless when it is still,
    Caught, held forever by the artist's skill.

Who will believe my verse in time to come
If in it I should dole out just deserts,
Judge, sentence, execute and to the tomb
Consign those friends of mine who blow their parts?
Far better if I put before your eyes
Imagined virtue, impossible graces,
And, the sweeter for my diction, all their lies,
That few might recognize their altered faces.
Time exacts its justice when with age
Too much frankness rides upon the tongue,
And all too often we express our rage,
Unable to enjoy the lovely lies of song.
    The poet's is a skilled revenge on time,
    Mastering it with rhythm and with rhyme.

Shall I compare thee to a summer's day
As if indeed the time were temperate,
Although the month's December and not May,
And wishes could transport you to that date?
Shall I invent a summer sun that shines
Less brightly since its very light is dimmed
By yours and in embarrassment declines,
Defeated though your beauty's candle's trimmed?
Alas, my love, your beauty soon must fade
And pay the grim taxation that it owes,
Until your life is gone and you a shade,
Quite gone to seed like everything that grows.
    But in that seed a promise dear I see,
    And I would love to snuggle up with thee.

Devouring time, blunt thou the lion's paws,
Consume as well all mortal men who breed,
Whose deeds defeat must snatch from victory's jaws,
And slow, then stop, the pulsing beat of blood.
What matter that they launch their mighty fleets
And sail upon your sea, O widow-making Time?
They savor victory's all too passing sweets
When shipwreck turns their triumph into crime.
So does the litany of lamentation grow,
A sort of victory by my mightier pen
Achieved, since Time its conqueror will allow
To tell his history to unborn men.
    How clearly life can seem to be quite wrong,
    Especially when we are very young.

A woman's face with Nature's own hand painted
Suffices to engage the lower passions,
With which we all are all too well acquainted;
No need to gild her lovely form with fashion.
Cruel time like mighty ocean rolling,
Surrounding one no matter where he gazes,
His hand upon the tiller scarce controlling
The deep impersonal sea that him amazes.
Why was such beauty ere created,
And why my eager passion on it doting,
When all our ardor must be soon defeated,
And all our everything bleakly come to nothing?
　　Inescapably evanescent pleasure
　　Is not where we will find a lasting treasure.

21

So it is not with me as with that Muse
That sweetly moves the bard to verse,
For thus she does us mortals use,
And we a fated fall seductively rehearse.
She'd have poets This with That compare,
Speak of our children as like gems,
Take from a million others a maiden rare,
And allow no taint to touch her hoisted hems.
Muse, let your dazzled poets write
Of peerless lips and laughing eyes so fair,
That by her looking on it the world is bright,
Her breath conferring vitality on air.
    This if it be done so very well
    Will not only please but also sell.

My glass shall not persuade me I am old
No matter that my face, a withered date,
Is not what one would willingly behold,
Except for penance, some sin to expiate.
Not like this do I dare come to thee,
This haggard face would scarcely win your heart.
The only way that you would turn to me
Is if my nature's covered up with art.
But is it wise for us to be so wary
Of the ravaged wrucks and graven wrinkles time will
Punish with? If of our nature we are chary,
We'd need a breed that never could fall ill.

    The youthful fair by passing time is slain,
    And none will have her beauty back again.

As an imperfect actor on the stage
To Tucson in an old Western repeats his part
And drives his fellow passengers to rage,
He takes so long to get the words by heart,
So I unscripted venture now to say
Our love does not enact a settled rite,
And is no talisman to stave off all decay,
Nor will our fragile love transmute, nor might.
There is a charm in native eloquence,
Words emerging from the virgin breast,
As if for lack of art there's recompense,
And truth its very self is then expressed.
    Wisdom is not confined to what is writ:
    That presupposes, and expresses, wit.

24

Mine eye hath played the painter and hath stell'd –
Or is it stalled? My hand stopped like my heart
As with an artist's eye your beauty I beheld
And trembled at the sacrilege of art.
What boots it if with supple hard-earned skill
One succeeds in telling only lies,
In making that which lives to be dead still,
And hold in one eternal gaze your eyes?
I am dissatisfied with all that I have done,
And yet high praise is coming now to me
Whose lunar art tells back the light of sun,
And thus is twice removed from lovely thee.
    I seek within the substitute of art
    What I cannot capture with my heart.

Let those who are in favor with their stars
Beg for autographs that they may boast
Of rubbing elbows in dimly intimate bars
With those whose celebrity is the most.
Why do we so desire to spread
The news of being briefly in the eye
Of fame, a fame that all to soon is buried,
Cast careless from attention like a die?
Each man engages in unnoticed fight,
When real thrust must parried be, and foiled,
A lifelong struggle which is never quite
Full won, though we can boast that we have toiled.
    O my vainglorious, still beautiful, beloved,
      May we by true, not fool's gold, be moved.

Lord of my love, to whom in vassalage
I in whom warm flesh and bone are knit,
Act wondrously, as to ambassage
In word and deed the vivifying spirit's wit.
The world in which I live is scarcely mine
Alone, and yet my mind embraces it,
Then gives it back in artful words to thee,
The vast and somehow awful givenness of it.
The love that us and all the stars is moving
Would be loved in each created aspect,
But is loved most by us when we are loving,
For then we hold it highest in respect.

    A spark of God is what I find in thee,
    And you may if you will find one in me.

Weary with toil, I haste me to my bed
And there retired acknowledge I am tired,
Hearing but buzzing confusion in my head,
That will not still till I am quite expired.
The labors of the day will still abide
When I at last am lying next to thee,
And in this burnished barge of bed so wide
No more in darkness daytime troubles see
But armed with you, to lidded eyes a sight
Unseen by day, in sun invisible to view,
Fondle the familiar and find it new
While fonder phantoms frolic in the night.
    Within the weary body, a sleeping mind
    May rest and strength for daytime dreaming find.

How can I then return in happy plight,
Weary from putting ardor to the test,
And contemplate the welcome of the night,
Where I by dreams alone will be oppressed?
The shining sun commands her waking reign,
But setting sets the stage for you and me.
I within your arms will not complain
Since I no longer am estranged from thee.
No need to deprecate the day's bright
Kingdom when stars cannot be seen in heaven,
Since they will come in series out at night,
Making of day to night an odd to even.

   So let our loving night be even longer,
    At dawn we'll rise so much the stronger.

When in disgrace with fortune and men's eyes
Defiant and alone I still will state
My case and in the stead of moaning cries
Enunciate acceptance of my fate.
I'll tell them how in dark despair my hope
Survives, I will not by misfortune be possessed,
But study stars as magnified by scope,
And find my troubles littler if not least.
Such resignation differs from despairing,
Nor does it mean denial of my state.
I see from ash the phoenix brightly rising,
To sing again before the heaven's gate.
    Misfortune that to plain men brings
    Sad wisdom comes as well to kings.

When to the sessions of sweet silent thought
We bring remembered glories of the past,
As dungy Job in his lost fortune sought
Some meaning other than an utter waste,
I'd rather seek to find in fortune's flow
Proportion of the daytime to the night,
A balancing of joy and baleful woe.
A vague but real purpose comes to sight.
And lamentation is quite soon foregone,
Although in dross there's little glittering ore.
Vicissitudes elicit involuntary moan,
And After seems to conquer its Before.
    Do you really want me as a friend,
      Knowing that you and I and all must end?

Thy bosom is endeared with all hearts,
Some alive, some among the dead,
Gone before you into nether parts
Where dwells the dust of those long buried.
Do not begrudge them now your memory's tear,
Who even to your faithless inner eye
Sometimes at moments must alive appear,
Although they all in graveyards still do lie.
It is the fate of those who briefly live,
Disport themselves awhile and then are gone,
That being taken from us still can give
The shock of presence when we are alone.
    Such somber thoughts apply as well to thee,
    And, indeed, do equally to me.

If thou survive my well-contented day
And run at dusk to find yourself a cover,
Then I a dim and spectral scene survey,
An unrequited and unquiet lover.
Abandoned, I will almost welcome time
To turn to paper and to inky pen
To capture you in language and in rhyme,
And make you known to who knows unknown men.
Thus does a poet avenge himself in thought,
His youth is conjured back in aching age,
And armies of the night by memory are brought
Back in all their moldering equipage.
    So I will with these rhyming lines still prove
    That love bereft of love imagines love.

33

Full many a glorious morning have I seen
With a blurred and bloody waking eye,
But still my reddened lens descried the green
About me, product of the sunlight's alchemy.
In azure sky the white clouds ride,
Unreal between the sun and earth. My face
In shadows lies when sun from me doth hide
Behind those nebulous travelers in disgrace.
But if that orb of fire would fully shine,
The shadow then would be upon my brow,
And I would with reluctance claim as mine
A landscape mottled less than it is now.
    A false observer chiaroscuro disdains:
    A maculate surface is the better for its stains.

Why didst thou promise such a beauteous day,
Then disappear within your copious cloak
And with adieu half-mumbled go your way,
Trailing a diabolic whiff of smoke?
The day begun with dawn is said to break,
Beauteous or otherwise, its morning face
Is what it is no matter that we speak
As if without our praise it's in disgrace.
It would as much sense make if we showed grief
That night is over, deeming lack of dark a loss.
Why should we not when daylight dies express relief
That in an absence of light our paths now cross?

    Nature waxes and wanes, gains or sheds,
    Independently of our words or deeds.

No more be grieved at that which thou hast done.
So what if you have wallowed in the mud,
Sinned when hid by night and in the sun,
And nipped all youthful promise in the bud?
Feel no remorse nor show regret at this.
To what could I your conduct negatively compare
Or say your crimes are in the least amiss
When I but say of you what you of me?
Nonsense needs as foil opposing sense,
Vice is not vice when virtue has no advocate,
And if there is no goal what means 'commence'?
Without the opposite of love, what's hate?

    In short, regret your faults and seek to be
    What you are not – no more than me.

36

Let me confess that we two must be twain
If we're to equal Samuel Clemens' one,
But even doubled or redoubled we'd remain
Trumped by his ice-cream suit alone.
Those who ape will all the more respect
The man; originals invite the spite
Of imitation which vainly seeks the effect
Simplicity conceals somehow to our delight.
What counts is, I am I and thee are thee,
Nor can I put it down to blushing shame
That you must come to mediocre me,
Take my imperfect hand and speak my proper name.
    When Gabriel blows and gathers men to sort,
      It is our unfeigned selves that must report.

As a decrepit father takes delight
In conjuring up his long departed youth,
And seems to overcome in thought the spite
Of time, finding dreams facsimiles of truth,
By doing so reveals his lack of wit.
His youth that paid the price of time, no more
Can for its portrait now unravaged sit,
But only show what youth had in its store.
The father who his age has thus despised
Has for his son no lesson then to give.
The evils of each age for each sufficed
And we should forward, not reversely, live.

    Decrepit father, in saying this to thee
    I realize that I but speak to me.

How can my Muse want subject to invent
When I turn bad so easily into verse?
Poetic invention is yet an excellent
Way one's rhyming folly to rehearse.
My Muse amuses her distant self with me,
Hoping perhaps that truth might come to sight,
And I turn from my shallow self to thee,
And with your love may find my burden light.
Nonetheless there is in this some worth
And I my Muse must often invocate
And by my efforts cause to issue forth
Some verse, as palm tree does its fruity date.
    I must be grateful for these dogstar days
      When I imperfectly announce your praise.

39

Oh how thy worth with manners may I sing,
Plucking heartstrings, but unmannered me
Can only hesitantly and sotto voce bring
Unmusical encomia to thee.
The poet must by measured number live,
And make dismembered sounds to sound as one,
The whole so framed and fashioned as to give
What may be music to himself alone.
Love, imperfection too can prove
To move the heeding heart, so by your leave
I shall in lines and stanzas sing our love
With purpose to delight, not to deceive.
    Though we are singly hung, made twain,
    We may hang separately, yet love remain.

Take all my loves, my love, yea, take them all,
Line them up and call them out before
Tribunals of disdain, but you must call
Them loves still – I only wish them more.
The received is shaped by her that him receives,
Made second-hand by hand that uses,
But such reception the receiver deceives,
Who cannot take what she so haughtily refuses.
Possession of my proper heart requires no thief.
Take me, and you but steal my poverty,
Nor lessen joy if in your grudging grief
You hearten even as you do me injury.

    This effort effortlessly confusion shows,
      Make of it what you will, my friends and foes.

41

Those pretty wrongs that liberty commits
Are larcenous because they wound the heart
Though they be done quite skillfully, as befits
Enactment of Ovid's amorous art.
The prey when half-pursued is surely won,
So I succumb though half-heartedly assailed.
I wonder if my mother's favorite son
Would love you half so much had he prevailed.
I count my losses blessings nor forbear
To say if amorous triumphs dreamt in youth
Were mine I'd not exchange this Here for There,
Though you for mine I cannot claim in truth.
    Such admission that I make to thee
    Is disingenuous and untrue to me.

That thou hast her, it is not all my grief,
Although in time's past I loved her dearly
And she of all my agonies was the chief:
She did not as much as I love nearly.
Her latest merry victim, God love ye,
Who think as I did once that you will win her,
Though I did think her then so much above me.
No matter, it is not me you'll trust but her.
If you should hold a mirror up to gain,
Prepare yourself for unreflected loss.
For you and she never shall be twain
Though she lie upon your shoulders like a cross.
    Into this world we come, one by one,
    And in the end we'll leave it all alone.

When most I wink, then do my eyes best see
But she reacts to winks as unrespected,
And turns from winking me to look at thee,
Whose open loving gaze at her's directed.
The windows of the soul are not so bright
When fluttering lids attempt their love to show.
They signal with an intermittent light
And signify that what is is not so.
The eye that God so artfully has made
Will function best when dawn brings on the day,
Not when the clouded sun is cause of shade.
Still, images visible but to memory stay.

    Thou art my sun who can see naught but thee,
    You cannot blame this blinking all on me.

44

If the dull substance of my flesh were thought,
And Descartes with his methodic way
Were right, who flesh and blood had brought
To mere res cogitans, I'd rather go than stay.
For how could mind in space be made to stand,
Or loving me get in warm touch with thee?
Methodic doubt despoils both sea and land,
Erases human hearts nor lets us bodily be.
The thought that you and I are chiefly thought,
And minds by thinking could make body gone,
Redefines the world that God has wrought,
Depriving lovers of their cause to moan.
  Disembodied mind with reason slow,
  Destroys the bodies mothers bore with woe.

The other two, slight air and purging fire,
Elementally in bodies do abide,
But water its level seeks with dumb desire
And runnelling earthward will with nature slide.
Fire, air, earth and water, after I am gone
Remain, and gone the love I felt for thee.
We each as single selves subsist alone
Or share in others' melancholy.
Nietzsche and the ancients held the world returned
And in some future I will once more love thee.
I wish this theory left me more assured,
But I diminish if time can multiply me.
    Browning's Duchess was too soon made glad,
    And repetition only made her sad.

Mine eye and heart are at a mortal war,
My pulsing blood, at odds with what my sight
Receives, brings it blinking to the bar
Of faithfulness, asserting its lawful right.
The sweets that now before us lovely lie
Undeniably appeal to hungry eyes,
This no one persuasively could deny,
Still glittering fool's gold only lies.
The jury that's within the heart impaneled
Attends what argument the loving heart
Will make, but its verdict's predetermined.
Eyes that crossed must in disgrace depart.

    Judicious loves will always play the part
    That they are cast for by their heart.

Betwixt mine eye and heart a league is took,
That not as two the two respect each other,
Nor would divorce if some disheartened look
Would then my looking heart be apt to smother.
Come integral to love's sweet feast,
Eye dependent on the pulse of heart,
Each as host and each as well as guest
Mutually enact a single part.
My eye and heart are one in one-ing love,
And you as half my heart unite with me
For I in being struck by thee now move
To be more surely wholly one with thee.
    Love, sole object of my hungry sight,
    Disarmed in arms now be my sole delight.

How careful was I, when I took my way.
Having dithered at the crossing, I then thrust
My hands into my pockets and did stay
On course, despite your usual lack of trust.
Places other than that in which we are
Give promise of an elsewhere joy where grief
Gives way and we indulge ourselves sans care,
But change is not a giver, it's a thief.
Go where we will the place within the chest
Remains unchanged, nor is there any art
To soothe immobile pain within the breast,
A thought that should attend us ere we part.
    Time tenses to the tune of fear
    That by leaving we must lose what's dear.

Against that time, if ever that time come,
When I can see like you all my defects
I'll surely quail to make of them a sum
And face the loss of all that love respects.
Such clairvoyant vision soon would pass,
Forgetfulness would lid my inner eye,
And bitter anguish that only briefly was
Would feel the pull of self-love's gravity.
Yet always the omniscient eye is here,
Toting up my all too earned desert.
Why like a rampant lion do I uprear
And occupy some self-redemptive part?
    If we will not observe God's lightened laws,
    The breaching of them misery will cause.

50

How heavy do I journey on the way
But in my head the image of the end
Lightens my burden, encouraging me to say,
My present foe might be a future friend.
A jeremiad intones its tale of woe
That, while true, must distance me from thee,
Did I not in oppressive darkness know
That in the end I shall be home with thee.
So must my present fortune urge me on,
Afford no niche in which a felon's hid,
By pressing on, I find relief in moan
Until it fades and I am at your side.
    In bringing all our woes before the mind,
    We're on the way to leaving them behind.

Thus can my love excuse the slow offense
And blame the one done with untimely speed,
Bid the doer to get him post-haste thence
And know the gnawing sorrow of love's need.
Fault in offenders we must surely find,
Blame one for speed, the other for being slow.
But when our passion's sheet fills swift with wind,
We would not only feel but feeling know.
A rabbit moves with shell-game's rapid pace
While tortoise but a single step has made,
Deliberately dividing the course to win the race:
Coursers thus can lose when running with the jade.
    Love, in offending me, continue slow,
    And I like lightning will to thee then go.

So am I as the rich whose blessed key
Is C, and like a tenor sing love's treasure,
You in the pits me on the stage survey,
And hearing feel with me my trebled pleasure.
Webs weave when truth's but spoken rare,
False words and falser mind do make a set,
Mendacious messages when typed are
Wafted out world wide upon the Internet.
Love encoded in the lover's chest,
Unseen, though having only love to hide,
Is virtually received by lovers blessed
And cherished with a real since private pride.
    Sung, said or coded, love has scope
    Sufficient to elicit her sweet sister hope.

53

What is your substance, whereof are you made,
That to love's gravity you will not tend,
And placed twixt sun and earth will make no shade
Nor to the borrowers of your beauty lend?
Caesar's coinage when thought counterfeit,
Like Caesar's wife to him and I to you,
Beneath suspicion, not above, is set,
And being used can never more be new.
Like the year, old love must cede to new,
So do not tears at loss of old love show
Though they may cleanse your heart till it appears
That newborn love in love's return you'll know.
    Love, let me be and not just act the part
    Of one whose habitat is in your heart.

O how much more doth beauty beauteous seem
When neighboring plainness does its contrast give;
She who's less endowed we then will deem
Not quite the maid with whom we'd choose to live.
Graying hair's not done away with dye
Nor paint to cheek gives hue of nature's roses.
She who's plain is loved less wantonly,
But to her lover's eye her soul discloses.
From beauty that consists of outward show
Unkind time will make all fairness fade,
While she who plain begins continues so,
But she retains the soul her goodness made.
    A passing phase is surface's beauty's youth,
    But time cannot destroy an inner truth.

Not marble nor the gilded monuments,
However solid, compete with fleeting rhyme.
The music of the poem encloses contents
That will not erode because of time.
In fleeting moments subsists the overture,
But solid is the state of masonry.
Such beauties seen or heard observers burn,
Each painlessly imprinted on their memory.
Evanescent music's eternity
Reaches the soul by asking ear for room,
As lovers seek in their posterity
A barrier to time and age that doom.
    0 love, see how love's children now arise,
    Objects both for ours and future eyes.

Sweet love, renew thy force; be it not said
That I view you with jaded appetite
Or that concupiscence, so much allayed,
Has left me shorn like Samson of my might.
But love, it's true that love can have its fill
And suffer sad effects from fullness,
Though sweetest love will mortals seldom kill,
Just blunt the edge of appetite with dullness.
Love, let us let our love in escrow be
A while; mere fondness may old love make new,
And we acquire a wiser eye to see
What earlier did not come fully into view.
    Let passion cede to a serener care,
    Which being less intense invites no stare.

Being your slave, what should I do but tend
Unto a state of mean, servile desire,
And having but obsequious coin to spend
Be out of pocket of that change that you'd requite.
Our love has reached its final Vesper hour
And I will soon be cast away by you,
For what was sweet has long since turned to sour
And we must bid each other fond adieu.
Would either of us earlier ever thought,
Or on the lifting wave of love suppose,
That all our fiery passion would be nought
But ashes, or These could ever be just Those?

    The ceaseless flight of love will not to will
    Respond, but flies, my love, for good or ill.

58

That god forbid that made me first your slave
And chattel, a puppet to afford you pleasure,
Which you awhile so ardently did crave,
Mere titillation to precede a sated leisure.
Another god has saved me from your beck,
And given back a long lost liberty,
The will to spurn commands I could not check
When shackled, and so did suffer injury.
One who was weak is now once more made strong,
And stronger still will be with passing time,
No longer shall I servilely belong
To one who turned my loving into crime.
    The harrowing of your imperious hell
    Is over, and I who ailed am now at last quite well.

59

If there be nothing new, but that which is,
And time by future promise unbeguiled,
We may not when we know it take amiss
This Now, past opportunity's only child.
My erstwhile love, come to the window, look
Where the lowing clouds beshroud the sun,
We've turned the last page of our book,
The tale that we've been writing is now done.
Observers of our outward acts could say
That as a portrait neatly fits its frame,
So we seem bordered and defined, but they
Cannot discern that Dorian's not the same.
    But could we quite regret the days
      When we exchanged love's dying praise?

Like as the waves make toward the pebbled shore,
Rolling from horizon without end,
Lose at our feet the force they had before,
Just so our love cannot its past contend.
Upon the fallen leaves a mottled light
Has with a borrowed gilt the dead leaves crowned.
So boxers, weary from too even fight,
In final rounds the gamblers all confound.
Ah love, my thoughts go back to our green youth,
Before the frown of failure lined the brow
And we would never guess the saddening truth
That is our shared and sole possession now.
    We rise like lovers and together stand,
      Taking each other by a spectral hand.

Is it thy will thy image should keep open
Season on prey that helpless day and night
Your dilatory hunting wounds with broken
Hearts, no longer pleasant to your sight?
If only I could also torture thee,
Your armored heart's protective shield pry
Loose, and make you vulnerable to me,
The subject, not the cause, of jealousy.
Thus do the small imagine being great,
And dream their anguish, which kept them long awake,
Wakes up another. But that were worse defeat,
Injustice done supposedly for justice' sake.
    The prisoner who dreamt for years of elsewhere,
    Ends by drawing to his jailer near.

Sin of self-love possesseth all mine eye
When in my glass I mimic your cruel part,
The afflicted in afflicting finding remedy
By sighing on a glassy unreflective heart.
If I took your part, would you take mine,
Call your abandoned self unto account
So that, become me for the nonce, you would define
How I indifference could surmount?
The sad drama we enact indeed
Has played with different actors since antiquity,
One could instance after instance read,
Proving you did not invent iniquity.
    Indifferent darling, no need to heed my praise,
    I'll keep it up no matter, down the days.

63

Against my love shall be as I am now,
All odds eventually alter, and that smile you've worn
Since first you made of me a slave, to clouded brow
Will turn, you'll find mere grayness in the morn,
Nor will you exercise your power at night,
For you will be the peasant and I the king.
Winter to my then recovered sight
Will sing with sweetness like the birded spring.
You must your fleeting strength still fortify,
Misfortune comes for certain like a knife
That severs fortune's thread and turns to memory
The dear dominance you thought would last for life.
    The melancholy truths are seldom seen
      Until too late; we miss them when we're green.

64

When I have seen by Time's fell hand defaced
A countenance that seemed immune to age,
Great beauty's an edifice quite razed,
Victim of the wrecking ball's full rage.
Pubescent girls will slowly beauty gain,
As oar by oar a boat makes for the shore,
But what is wanted may the wanter harm,
Nor could the maid imagine what's in store.
When with passing time she's reached that state
The process will continue, to decay.
Greybeards weighed down by life must ruminate,
And pass their dwindling time away.
    It is not given mortal man to choose
    A mortal love he will not one day lose.

Since brass, nor stone, nor earth, nor boundless sea
Are metaphor enough to catch your power,
No more would I to buzzing bee make plea
To mimic an apt companion for the flower.
Some things are best expressed straight out.
To what could we compare our single days,
What improving image find for milk or stout,
What word to hide the way that love decays?
Mixed things only, things that lack
Simplicity, have essence that is hid.
Elemental things, nor front nor back,
But all at once are given and metaphor forbid.
    Your simple single sameness has such might,
    Your light is what makes other things be bright.

66

Tired with all these, for restful death I cry,
Remove the weight beneath which I was born,
Do not recall the days of jollity
When all the rest I had for thee foresworn.
Remembered times of love are now misplaced,
I think of naught but that I'm strumpeted
And by your graceless folly am disgraced,
My heart torn out, for life I am disabled.
My unkind friends invoke authority
That wounded love prepares another skill,
Uncomplicated, honest, all simplicity,
Which offers all too sure escape from ill.
    When mine, you were in truth already gone,
    Now I must start to heal myself alone.

Ah, wherefore with infection should he live
Who shows the world such rank impiety
And would in selfish rapture but achieve
Defiance of all decent society.
A passion that does not hold itself in check
Is imitation of love's native hue.
They that satisfaction only seek
Are lustful louts and far from lovers true.
Within the pulsing beat of blood there is
Such madness coursing through the veins
That what is hers he would have roughly his,
And lose the goal that he but seeming gains.

    The fresh young hope of love in violence had
    Suffers an alteration from good to bad.

68

This is his cheek the map of days outworn,
What was roseate is only ashen now
And youth that was to such smooth beauty born
Now wears time's runnels on its brow.
Thus we imagine noble lovers dead,
Who did in time see beauty age away,
For teeth will go and hair fall from the head,
Thus learned that none remain si toujours gai.
The beauty that by outer eye is seen
Is false when taken for a beauty true,
The soul acquires an everlasting green
Which with age remains forever new.
    Youth had best in soul its virtue store,
    That can in future time be as in yore.

69

Those parts of thee that the world's eye doth view
Differ from those that only to the mind
Display the beauty that is virtue's due
And will to more discerning minds commend.
With outer beauty you were by nature crowned,
But inner beauty little to nature owes.
The merely found its finder will confound,
And when lost as merely luck is shown.
The inward look that is the power of mind
Discerns within the quality of deeds,
Knows virtue's beauty is another kind,
And lilies that fester smell worse than weeds.
    Sweet beauty that is merely outer show,
    By chance has come and by dire fate will go.

70

That thou art blamed shall not be thy defect
Nor can you lose what makes you truly fair.
Carping critics who feign that it is suspect
Would rail against the given gift of air,
Of which they only shallowly approve.
All alters with the altering of time
But to the kinder eye of faithful love
A fading beauty still is in its prime.
One single light illumines all our days
And by its energy all we see is charged
With that which rightly earns our praise
And makes the praiser's soul to be enlarged.
 The gambler does, win, place or show,
 Believe that chance bestows, but does not owe.

No longer mourn for me when I am dead
Nor dirges play nor toll the dismal bell,
For when in earth I'm laid at last to bed
My spirit will in a better country dwell,
Where then what is will be as if it's not,
And what is not will be again. 'Tis so,
For there is that which cannot be forgot
But rises out of reach of tearful woe.
Why would the poet seek to catch in verse
Our deeds if we were only drying clay
And did not in our lives by acts rehearse
A drama that resists mortal decay?
    Our going would elicit only moan
    If we were wholly gone when we are gone.

O lest the world should task you to recite
Some lines expressive of our mighty love,
Deny mere words such fire can capture quite,
Or cogent syllogisms ever prove.
Do golden nuggets in the roadway lie,
Or rain forests sweat upon the sandy desert?
Say rather it's your mystery that I
Do love and find in it your deepest import.
No telling could express the sense of this,
That by expression only seems untrue,
Because ineffably to me it is
The unseen essence that is truly you.
    Sensible speech the sensed can body forth
    But leaves unsaid your true and hidden worth.

That time of year thou mayest in me behold
When drying leaves from sapless branches hang
And in the air there's promise of the cold,
And southward flee the birds that lately sang
When sun stood at meridian of day,
Though tending as it must unto the west,
As season steals the prior season away,
And all the wintering world lies down to rest.
Nature is a self-consuming fire
That in its glory is a gorgeous lie,
Leaping ever higher only to expire
As you and I will, darling, by and by.
      Victory goes to him who's proven strong
      But cannot wear its laurel very long.

But be contented. When that fell arrest
Is made and you are tumbreled swift away,
The capital demand upon your head may interest,
But none can make the dropping blade to stay
And as it falls, your life in fleet review
Will pass before thine eyes to prove to thee
This punishment so cruel is over due.
In this you are no different from me.
In pain and squalling we are given life
And when it's finally taken we are dead
Some other way if not by falling knife
And being gone will not be long remembered.
    Our passing life a dusty truth contains:
    Eventually nothing but dust remains.

So you are to my thought as food to life,
As to my flattened soles is solid ground:
When I am sore beset by bitter strife,
Armed and at my side you're always found.
So will it be, so was it e'er anon.
The coinage of your courage is my treasure,
I do not fear I'll ever be alone
Or quite bereft of your companioned pleasure.
Even absent you are present to my sight
As though you could be conjured by a look,
And in your presence I still take delight,
Remembering past pleasures that we took.
    The pagan cried, O seize the day!
    But pagan and his days have passed away.

Why is my verse so barren of new pride,
So devoid of sweet surprise to change
Your heart, prompting you to put aside
Indifference and hear familiar song as strange?
As is my verse so is my love the same,
Its usual flower smells to you like weed,
Whose prolific seed deserves the name
Of him from whom they passionately proceed.
But love, my rhymed address is aimed at you
And must commend itself sans argument.
What is old cannot again be new,
Though its reiteration is not spent.

 What is new, repeated is made old,
 But can with old pride still be told.

The glass will show thee how thy beauties wear,
A land too cultivated is laid waste
Nor can the nearly barren bushes bear
A fruit that still is sweet to jaded taste.
My limbs and face as well their age will show,
So you and I repair to common memory,
To images recalling what we once did know,
Fixed in the past's untrue eternity.
Your face held in my hands does not contain
What no longer in the present I can find,
Yet you are lodged within my conscious brow
And can delight, if not the senses, mind.
    A page's surface will to a scholar's look
    Pay back the hidden contents of the book.

So oft have I invoked thee for my Muse
That I amuse myself by making verse,
Which written down for any reader's eye,
Would to the four winds our privacy dispense.
It is impossible aloud to sing
And stay the words that to a strange ear fly,
Borne publically upon song's wing
And when common lose their private majesty.
I might of course unpublished verse compile,
Its message to be heard by none but thee,
Encode it in a cabalistic style,
But it would cease true poetry to be.

    The undeciphered cannot much advance
    My cause or penetrate elected ignorance.

Whilst I alone did call upon thy aid,
Others content to bank upon God's grace,
My aspirations over time decayed,
Leaving me in this too desolate place.
Unheeded, the logic of my argument
Drained ink and language from my pen,
Till I both help and helper must invent.
I shall not call upon thy aid again.
Once you blithely said. "But say the word,
But ask, my friend, and I shall surely give."
Such assistance you once swore to afford,
That I might live quite well, not merely live.
    You were too quick to smile and say
    Such words, but then with words alone you pay.

Oh how I faint when I of you do write,
Oblivion obscures thy very name
Which I cannot recall, try as I might,
So fragile in my heart was thy brief fame.
When only written of a person is,
But nominal existence does she bear,
And her reality is only his
Who makes her on the page in lines appear.
The castoff on the sea is kept afloat
And on the pulsing deep is glad to ride
On borrowed artifice to any boat
But soon, gone artifice, gone boat, gone pride.
     You were here but now you've gone away,
     Like an extracted tooth that showed decay.

Or I shall live your epitaph to make,
Or no graven words when flesh is rotten
Will from death its lethal stinger take,
Remembered and rememberer forgotten.
The sense of loss that we at funerals have
Sometimes obscures that we as well must die.
How odd that standing by another's grave
The thought does not occur that thus we'll lie.
And yet in chiseled stone, also in verse,
We fashion words that later will be read,
And by our grave words we rehearse
The all too pending time when we'll be dead.
    That said, I get a grip upon my pen
    And celebrate your virtues to unborn men.

I grant thou wert not married to my Muse –
At incestuous unions gods askance will look, –
But whether you are usufruct or use,
You are the inspiration of my book.
In your ambience I give the world a hue
Itself has not and this patina praise
As if creation were born by it anew
And adds another to its seven days.
Will a world suffice that is devised
By art and dares its office to nature lend?
He who with images overly sympathized
Could lose sight of his original friend.

    It is a paradox that art when used
    Ends with underlying nature abused.

I never saw that you did painting need,
Or that your face must be in mud pack set,
Cosmetics nature's lily far exceed,
And love prefers to be in nature's debt.
A penciled sketch that would a scene report,
And, intermediary, attempt to show
It by hatched and single lines, falls short –
Real objects in the real scene do grow
Apace. Were we to pictures to impute
Reality, we would quite soon by nature dumb
Be stilled, before its majesty standing mute,
Our silence become the silence of the tomb.

    The world that dies before our worlding eyes
    Out-marvels all that we by art devise.

84

Who is that says most, which can say more
Than that All is still far less than you?
Superlatives plucked from our expressive store
Are simple truths that grew and grew and grew.
Far better that I who on your beauty dwell
Should not with More and Most enhance your glory,
But let thy lovely lineaments simply tell
Their unadorned and quite sufficient story.
The saintly monk who ponders Holy Writ
Does not by reading make, but finds, it clear.
Interpolations expressive of subtle wit
Soon lose their sense and go not anywhere.
    Hyperbole is sophistry's great curse,
      Which trying to better, only makes things worse.

My tongue-tied Muse in manners holds her still,
Whose liquor measured by the cups before me piled
Intoxicates and thus she drives my quill
Erratically until the page is filled.
I pluck from out the lexicon of words
The choice, using last the best: Amen.
Sobeit, I tell the Muse who oft affords
A liquid better than ebon ink to pen.
In wine, it's said, the sot may say what's true,
And in his cups may drink a nectar more
Conducive to express undoubled you
Than when he saw you sober hours before.
    So do not reckon it my disrespect
    If I should pause to feel the wine's effect.

Was it the proud full sail of his great verse
That with its windy bloviation won you,
Like Cleopatra whom passion did inhearse
As bosom- feeding adder fatter grew?
Bards tell many a lie and worse they write,
But seldom are found out until they're dead,
When at last their lying tongue, in night
Of death, is stilled, their fame leaves most astonished.
But he will doubtless charm you as a ghost,
Your vulnerable love-addled intelligence
Hearing only heroic couplets in his boast.
Ah, how I wish that he were quickly hence.
    A poet, my dear, has a seductive line;
    If I were one I'd swiftly make you mine.

Farewell! Thou art too dear for my possessing.
Shock shook me when I read the estimate
Of payment for your ultimate releasing
From the mechanics' clutches at a date determinate.
You were a good old car. I'm granting
That, of my loyalty more than deserving,
Despite the many things in which you're wanting.
Item. Your unnerving habit of sudden swerving;
Your cloudy glass and dented fenders; no knowing
From your gauge amount of fuel, mistaking
Empty for half full. Your faults are growing.
Item. The black smoke you're always making.

    Exhausted car, your tires could not be flatter;
      You're graveyard bound, but so am I. What matter?

When thou shalt be disposed to set me light,
Even above the range of your cold scorn,
My going caused by neither quarrel nor fight,
Or by my love explicitly foresworn,
A time will come when I shall be acquainted
With blithe indifference to our dim story.
A brow lifted, a nostril aquiver as if attained
By acrid smoke from my burnt glory.
There is a law that the disdainer too
Eventually shall be disdained. To thee
Some future love may these sad honors do,
Nor do I mourn that it will not be me.

    The risk a lover takes is to belong
    To one who's like to do him grievous wrong.

Say that thou didst foresake me for some fault,
For some unwitting but still felt offense,
How might I with a word your turning halt,
And not further offend by a confused defense?
That I whom you did love could do you ill,
Or my fixed breast be subject to such change,
Escapes the tethered power of my will.
Could half my soul be to my soul so strange?
Excuses come too quickly to the tongue
But not from where the deepest love does dwell.
Arise. I'm wronged, but will not call you wrong:
Truth becomes untrue if I should tell.

    Not with you, but with myself debate
    Rages, yet love will never turn to hate.

Then hate me when thou wilt, if ever, now,
Let me take up forthwith the cross,
Blameless beneath it let my shoulder bow,
And let my wounded heart sink low with loss.
But I'm not granted such dramatic sorrow,
An outer show of my consuming woe,
Nor dare I hope that with a swift tomorrow,
I might with ease your doubting overthrow.
A shoe is forced to fit its maker's last,
Nor could upon its fashioner turn in spite,
No more could I acquire another taste
Than you, though fickle you it seems just might.
　　I go enveloped in enduring woe
　　And grieve the more that this is ever so.

Some glory in their birth, some in their skill,
But I shall glory in love's restoring force
That found me by the roadside fallen ill,
As one thrown by a not too faithful horse.
Love lifted me from pain to sweetest pleasure,
Cushioned me with comfort and dear rest,
And laid me long your beauty as a measure,
Taught me standards by which to judge the best.
The depths from which your love has rescued me
With graceful ease and scarcely any cost,
Brought to heights undreamt before by me,
Recalled, brings triumph without the need to boast.
    The potter in his hands some clay doth take,
    And by his art will his own image make.

But do thy worst to steal thyself away,
No distancing could make you less all mine,
Or by departing negate that you must stay
Within the heart that ever more is thine.
Never by real or by imagined wrongs
Could what's begun in me come to an end.
This heart forever to you alone belongs,
Abandoned, it would no less on you depend.
True love exists both in the heart and mind
And never could to its own self give lie,
Or by whatever loss could fail to find
Your presence, if you should go, if you should die.
    On my escutcheon there will be no blot
    That comes from saying that that which is, is not.

So shall I live, supposing thou art true
Doubting you have another face than face
You turn to me as when your love was new
As Eve's for Adam in that original place.
The honest organ that is your lovely eye
Bears not a look that would or could e'er change
And you and I have lived a history
That makes for us what is familiar strange.
Love does not rule by altering decree,
But would its clients ever faithful dwell,
That what was, is still, may ever be,
Though only to your heart will I this tell.
    Love unseen by others still will grow,
      And flourish with no need for outer show.

That thou has power to hurt, and will do none
The wounds you yet inflict will never show.
My love honed keener on your heart of stone
Bears marks dripped in by waters slow.
One learns to settle for the outer graces
Dispensed, God knows, at very little expense;
We learn to love unloved with no long faces,
As if a pretty show concealed an excellence.
My heart that once responded to the sweet
Solace of your love now sours and dies,
The harshest judge would not pronounce it meet
That humbled love be robbed of dignity.
    One looks for excellence in your deeds,
    As one in search of flowers finds only weeds.

How sweet and lovely dost thou make the shame
That plainness feels, confronted by a rose
That's recognized no matter what its name,
As accidents one essence will enclose.
Remember, love, in short December days
Those lengthy summers when you and I'd disport,
And gamboling, exchange much mutual praise,
Cloudless sunshine the only weather report.
Our year has aged and you and I have got
Through fall and into winter, but I love thee
The more nor will consider age a blot
Since still it is your loving heart I see.
    There's public law and there is privilege,
     Which binds us ever and will to time's last edge.

Some say thy fruit is youth, some wantonness,
Some another intramural sport.
Ah, they know you not: your faults are less
Than they suppose, for only as a last resort
Do you resort to cheating, palm Ace or Queen
Adroitly so that uncaught you are esteemed,
Vice concealed and only virtue seen;
You are not what you are by many deemed.
One day some inadvertence will betray
You, and your sinless countenance translate
To sinful wantonness, sweep away
What hides for now your future woeful state.
    But which of us is truly of the sort
    We're taken for in a benign report?

How like a winter has my absence been,
A season that refrigerates the year,
No bed in bloom anywhere to be seen
And under snow is buried that place where,
In ever changing nature's warmer time,
We did by ever giving love our love increase
And, glorying in our lifetime's prime,
Lost the sense of 'cease' and of 'decrease'.
Out of hibernation now, to me
Returns the season in which the sweetest fruit
Is gathered and brought by me to thee,
And songbirds in the trees no more are mute.
    Oh how my heart expands with summer cheer,
      When rescued from my winter I see you drawing
        near.

From you have I been absent in the spring
When fields are cultivated and farmers trim
The vine to make it more fecund, each thing
Of nature when nurtured more by man repays him
Hundredfold but I have been where smell
Of flowers comes not from nature, where the hue
Of painted cheek is such that all can tell
It's counterfeit, and fruit that's seedless grew.
No facsimile competes with white
As found in nature, nor green nor gold nor rose,
Nor can a fashioned beauty much delight,
Your attributes must triumph over those.
    And now I learn that while I was away,
    Like mice sans cat, all you did was play.

The forward violet thus did I chide,
Do not preen upon your purple smells
As on accomplishments your petaled pride
Explained, and you might ask admirers to dwell
Upon your beauty as if your art had dyed
You into loveliness, as skillful hand
Transforms with tricks and oil a maiden's hair,
Causing what of itself would lie to stand.
Your vanity will bring you to despair,
Along with all your lovers, for both
Mistake the source from which your scented breath
Accompanies your shy or prideful growth,
Which when withheld must lead us on to death.
    Violet, your native beauty is what we see,
    Not what any art bestowed on thee.

100

Where art thou, Muse, that thou forget'st so long
Thy long mute slave who, try as he might,
Cannot without your whisper sing a song.
My iambic feet stumble without your light,
It is only your inspiration that redeems
For me the name of poet, and I am spent
Without dispensing what my love esteems:
All cogent nexus is lacking to my argument.
When I the rolls that list the poets survey,
My eye can find no single entry there,
No name your help did not save from decay,
Nor any self-made singer anywhere.
    Muse, your ministrations give me life,
    Without them I should fall upon my knife.

101

O truant Muse, what shall be thy amends
When I have sung of her whose hair is dyed,
Of her whose crusted beauty now depends
On quaint concoctions by name undignified?
For should I of that painted lady say
That she is one on whom each eye is fixed,
And that no lover could ever be so lax
As not to praise her, then lies with truth are mixed.
No more I'll sing but I will be quite dumb,
Until again I'm troubadour for thee.
My strings are still, my voice is like the tomb:
Though once called lovely, she can no longer be.
    By art the poet is someone knowing how
    To sing of anything, but I'll not now.

My love is strengthened, though more weak in seeming,
My sinews tense far more than will appear,
My fortitude is weak beneath esteeming,
And I am mocked and laughed at everywhere.
Once I knew the season of the spring,
When I was wont to sing my lovely lays,
But now my voice is far too weak to sing,
Unless it sings the dying of the days.
You'll find me quite inaudible now,
Dark clouds have turned my day to naught,
No longer on my brittle leafless boughs
Do birds with feathered arias all delight.
    In desert wastes the dry and thickened tongue
    Is incapable of any song.

Alack what poverty my Muse brings forth,
Her strict Franciscan vow permits no pride
Nor does she longer count it of much worth
To sing of you and of your beauty beside.
It is as if, not I, but this pen must write
And seek to trace in ink the memory of your face.
But without a higher inspiration it is quite
Unable, and scratches me to itching disgrace.
Around me bend the waiting ears of men
Who know that if I could once more sing well,
All my tender notes would tendered tend
To that mute mystery that none may tell.
   The model for the painter once did sit
   That he might find her soul where God had put it.

104

To me, fair friend, you never can be old.
Or my watch has stopped or, looked at blurry-eyed,
Will not reveal true time. To eye more cold,
You'll seem bereft of all that was your pride.
This lifeless earth so many times has turned
Since that far dawn in which your youth was seen,
The solitary sun has daily burned
Above and changed to brown what once was green.
Yet on the bridal finger of your hand
That ring of gold is as it was perceived
When you with me did at the altar stand
And pledged a troth which never was deceived.
    Think of babies that might have gone unbred,
    And never would think of us when we are dead.

105

Let not my love be called idolatry,
Nor hyperdulia either, when I affection show
That was and is and ever more shall be,
For heart to heart must whisper ever so.
Were we but instances of human kind,
Possible, but generic, excellence,
We might with any others be confused
Without a jot of our dear difference.
There is in blood an urgent argument
Far deeper, Love, than that which rides on words,
Which with cordial cogency is spent
And its unique and personal proof affords.
    Ah love, it is when we are most alone
      That you and I most perfectly are one.

106

When in the chronicle of wasted time
My deeds unwittingly record what wights
Must find an all too prosy rhyme,
Worthy of doleful countenanced errant knights.
I am not much when I am at my best,
Any sun may seem to cloud my brow,
And though in speech I'd love to have expressed,
You'll find me mute, as mute I still am now.
Still, men ignore prosaic prophesies
And marvel at the fact of your preferring
Wasted me who in your biased eyes
Is pleasing, for even crows in cawing sing.
    There's this redeems even my dullest days,
      That though unworthy, I still receive your praise.

Not mine own fears, not the prophetic soul,
Not even the devils who at noonday come
In hope Satanic malice may control
My deeds and lead unwitting to my doom
Can alter this that I have all along endured,
And however feebly done, what promises presage,
And I however anxious am assured
That love begun in youth persists in age.
The reader who half-wittedly peruses Time,
To which he half-wittedly subscribes,
Should seek not in such prose for any rhyme:
He'll only find the lies of dribbling scribes.
    Look not in any print for monument
    To that long love in which my life's been spent.

What's in the brain that ink may character,
As in their watery passage squids will spirit
Off what's writ in water; what could register
At all as does your warm expressive merit?
There is in every man a spark divine,
That being unsame we somehow are the same;
It is this spark of mine that unto thine
Would fire what love can only feebly name.
Can love decline from case to lower case,
Like mortal hero degenerate with age,
Or like a wandering scholar's eye lose place
And wander aimless all about the page?
   We who were in inspiration bred
    Will cool and end in coldness of the dead.

O never say that I was false of heart,
Such charge you must in truth soon qualify.
True, sailors will from any port depart,
Whispering to maidens their strange and honeyed lies
And I, you know, far over the world have ranged –
When I was young, then later and now again,
And in the wechsels of the world exchanged
More than money and on my soul's the stain.
Through all my wandering only you have reigned,
The single truth that pulses in my blood;
Your purity will make my soul unstained,
So I though bad can recognize the face of good.
    Few answer we are told love's call,
     Though it's addressed to one and all.

Alas, 'tis true I have gone here and there,
My feet have taken me to where the view
Is famous and to places rightly dear
To those for whom they're old, not new.
There comes with travel this plain truth,
That journey far below or yet above,
All travel takes us farther from our youth
But brings us back like pilgrims to our love.
There lies ahead a grimmer journey's end,
However slow the godly mills may grind,
When hairless, toothless, deaf, without a friend,
We'll be within our lonely selves confined.
    Sometimes it seems that life was at its best
    When toothless we suckled at our mother's breast.

O for my sake do you with fortune chide,
And argue lest the merits of my deeds,
Are offset by the guilt that sins provide,
For fecundating evil evil breeds.
Exiled Cain departed with his brand,
Because in wrath his brother he subdued,
Bringing down but once his murderous hand,
Which done, the moment could not be renewed.
The cup we take and from it freely drink
May hold a tonic or a dread infection.
Oh who has erred and did not after think,
Bring back that moment for my quick correction?
    The moment, love, when I encountered thee,
    I would not change, for it changed me.

112

Your love and pity doth th'impression fill,
As I gaze drugged upon your dentist brow,
And I can feel no pain though I am ill
And will your drill its entry now allow.
A numbed jaw quite pointlessly will strive
To feel the probing of the numbed-too tongue.
How odd insensate to remain alive,
As when the soul becomes quite dead to wrong.
Such thoughts accompany dental care,
For mind goes on when it is lost to sense
And in the isolation of the soul we are
Wealthy still, though tongue's unable to dispense.
    Technicians in their shiny labs have bred
    Concoctions to make us while still living dead.

113

Since I left you, mine eye is in my mind,
My hand is on my heart and as I feel about,
My clouded eye by murky mind made blind
Keeps looking in and never will look out.
Still my hand is steadied by my heart,
Reposing there as key does in its latch.
Like heart mind's a metonymous part
And withers what world its reaching serves to catch.
Some say that heart confers a better sight
Than mind, accepting as it will each creature,
And in its red and warmish almost night
Discerns by touch each being's telltale feature.
    Though I be false in all my thoughts of you,
    I never in my heart could be untrue.

Or whether doth my mind, being crowned with you,
Become immune to others' flattery,
Finding only false what might be true,
Clouded by the logic of love's alchemy?
A system's named after our power to ingest,
But what it feeds upon it won't resemble;
That power of powers shall be accounted best
That will things as they are but reassemble.
The eye flows outward in its seeing
Nor ever eats its distant object up,
Just so the shape of wine ends by agreeing
With the embracing inner shape of cup.

    To seek to be like God is Original Sin,
      But sinful man did not as such begin.

These lines that I before have writ do lie
Upon a page that yellowed is the dearer,
Afford an answer to the question Why,
Which with time's passage becomes clearer.
Substance must suffer many accidents,
And vassals will attach themselves to kings,
But read here now my linear intent,
Which understood, reveals many things.
Without slaves there is no tyranny,
The very worst is needed by the best,
And certitude its opposite, uncertainty,
And what is movement if there be no rest?
  I have shaped my thoughts on love just so,
  Which pondered seedlike in your mind will grow.

Let me not to the marriage of true minds
Or of false bodies equivocate on love.
The common word no common meaning finds,
No more can water what's indelible remove.
Consider how the federal German mark
Will fluctuate, by currencies be shaken,
Its bite quite toothless, though its Teutonic bark
Unnerves those who by its roar are taken.
The primal winds will blow with fulsome cheeks,
As if the last and ultimate trump had come,
But there are blossoms hidden in the weeds
Which spell for pretense only surer doom.
    One thing Euclid always failed to prove,
    Was that one who loves is also loved.

117

Accuse me thus: that I have scanted all,
Have held back that with which I might repay,
Have left unheeded every debt when called,
And so an undiminished treasure have today.
There may be those with more divided minds,
Who bargain broadly and always set things right,
Who scatter substance to the stripping winds
And are made visible to a crowded sight.
But I have kept my hoard pressed down
And running over, let pennies accumulate,
Ignored all creditors, defied their frown
And for your love have courted all their hate.
    My misered heart is only meant to prove
    The growing interest of singular love.

118

Like as to make our appetites more keen,
More prompt to answer blood's dark urge,
We capitulate to powers unseen,
So as from conscience its full sting to purge.
There lies in loving thus no sweetness,
When mind will yield to every sway of feeling,
Not in this will you and I find meetness,
Succumbing to the simple lack of needing.
For mind before the senses must anticipate
The road by which our honor is assured,
Or else we'll end up in a sorry state
Where the soul of man is never cured.
> So let me seem though cold more truly true,
> And give myself by mind's impulse to you.

What potions have I drunk of Siren tears,
What drugs unwisely have I took within,
As if by artificial means to numb the fears
And by succumbing feign that I should win?
Our selves consist of deeds we have committed,
And if sometimes we've done what we should never,
How like us then our claim the shoe is fitted
To another's foot and health consists of fever.
Our task is difficult, we must be true,
Nor can we, getting worse, be said to better,
The older got, the harder we renew,
And shrunken are unlikely to grow greater.
   'Tis difficult, constrained to be content,
    And by false freedom all our substance spent.

120

That you were once unkind befriends me now,
And having felt the opposite now feel
As bowman who extends the string and bow,
But only fire can turn our iron to steel.
Modest acts have oft foundations shaken,
As instants are the elements of time.
The little wrong, the evil turn once taken,
Evolves swiftly from venial to mortal crime.
Despite my sullied state I have remembered,
If not a strike-out, then several early hits.
Even toughened I to you once tendered
A love I now but feel in starts and fits.

    The broad road entered exacts a cruel fee,
    That takes its toll till bell will toll for me.

Tis better to be vile than vile esteemed,
Though sometimes one's esteemed for vile being;
The common fault is that the vile is deemed
Virtuous, exposing whitened sepulchers for seeing.
The inner self's invisible to eyes,
Save when the wounded heart pumps out its blood
So that the more discerning critic spies
The evil that hid beneath the skin of good.
We mediocre men would to our level
Reduce the public hero, refuse to own
His merit, and see not pane but only bevel,
When our mirrored self reflectively is shown.
    Appearance and reality struggle to maintain
    Their balance, but appearance alas will reign.

Thy gift, thy tables, are within my brain,
And pool is played upon my cushioned memory,
Balls that take their cue from stick remain
Stopped in the moment's false eternity.
But let them be within my brain or heart,
Thy gifts will cordially subsist
Where neither rust nor moth has part
And will by prowling thieves be safely missed.
Beside the table I now this cue stick hold,
And count upon the wire my mounting score,
Your smile impels my wish to play so bold,
To clear the table of everything but you.
  The metaphor of games applies to thee
  As much as, win or lose, it does to me.

No, Time, thou shalt not boast that I do change,
Boasting is unworthy of you. You might
Observe that physically it's passing strange
To stand stock still while going out of sight.
Willy-nilly all things change: we admire
A man, not because he's young or old,
Not because he's tossed about by his desire,
But for his timeless virtue timely told.
Canute tried by his fiat to defy
The laws of motion and of time, but past
Hours will roll upon the shore, lie
Tenseless there, drained of lenten haste.
    I change places, move from A to B,
    Only, love, to be right next to thee.

If my dear love were but the child of state,
Plato's republican bairn unfathered
By its father whom it is taught to hate,
Then I must cherish the gift from our hearts
    gathered,
Since our contingent love is yet no accident,
Some sportive character that freely falls
From outside on us, as if it were like discontent
Or other mood. My heart to your heart calls.
Let him who seeks analysis of love a heretic
Be called. He'd parse to moments the long hours
Lovers linger in embrace, make politic
Consist of letters and, counting drops, miss showers.
    There's need perhaps for daylight saving time,
    But lovers would increase the night in any clime.

Were't aught to me I bore the canopy,
Footstool, scepter or other item honoring
A temporal glory, I'd know that under eternity
That which builds us up can cause our ruining.
Far from me to fawn and curry favor
With those whose garments crumpled are and rent,
Their crowns awry, quaffing a bowl whose savor
Is scarce tasted before it's wholly spent.
Yet there is that which lasts in mortal heart,
Breaks the chains of slaves and makes them free,
A scintilla divina in which thou art
Divine, a spirit that upward flies with thee.
    The body's animate because of soul,
      And its sweet governance lies in control.

O thou, my lovely boy, who in thy power
Thy father sees his swiftly passing hour,
Finding in all the unspoiled good that shows
Proof that an angel always with you goes,
A guardian sent to save you from eternal wrack,
Who if you stray will cry out, 'No, go back!'
I bequeath to you a feeble skill,
And mortal flesh, as if to sire's to kill,
And yet you are my melancholy pleasure,
No moth or rust can touch your inner treasure.
    Transmitting life can double portent be,
    So may I see some of my self in thee.

In the old age black was not counted fair,
Nor did evil dare to take of good the name,
Though every son and daughter to Adam heir
Bore on his soul the mark of Adam's shame.
In weakness we look back to primal power,
Before the radiant creature hid his face
And primal parents were turned from out their bower,
Bearing, as all they'd bear, the first disgrace.
And so it is that white is counted black,
That is its kingdom now, to seem,
And men puff up with pride because they lack
The basis and the claim of true esteem.
    The race of Adam forgets its fated woe,
    And wanders where it should not want to go.

How oft, when thou, my music, music plays
I wish my ears could capture all the sounds
With which you freight the air, but as thou swayest,
I will read your hips. So song confounds
The senses and I to sight from hearing leap,
Deaf as a post, my ear's cupped by my hand,
Not every seed that's sowed will mankind reap,
But those they do in stubbled fields may stand.
Songs are unheard by those in deafened state,
So too the scarcely audible crackle of chips –
All that is lost on me, and though your gait
Is fetching, sweetheart, I would read your lips.
    My darling, when I pucker up like this,
    I crave the muted music of your kiss.

The expense of spirit in a waste of shame,
The tragic forfeiture of grace to lust,
The maddened moth's attraction to the flame,
And my betrayal of your unearned trust –
Such unoriginal proofs of sin seem straight
From hell, innocence now lost, that once was had.
The fickle fish when hungry take the bait,
So serpent's bite will make the reason mad.
Would that this tragic business were not so,
But since it is I pray that at extreme
Of life the blessed unction will the woe
My life deserves dissolve into a dream.
    When one has lived but not lived well,
    Mercy alone preserves his soul from hell.

My mistress' eyes are nothing like the sun,
For they will rise at dawn in sunset red
When she to table comes all wrapped in dun
And hair wound round the curlers on her head.
Some cream has left her face all streaked with white,
There are no dimples on her splotchy cheeks,
There is, alas, so little to delight
The eye – or nose, for she of smoke still reeks.
When man knows woman he must also know
That she has depths no husband wants to sound,
His wisdom is to let such defects go
Unnoticed, since he too stands on shaky ground.
    The maiden had such springlike beauty rare,
    Her later self can scarce to it compare.

Thou art as tyrannous, so as thou art,
Like tyrants all who when they would be cruel
Rain bitter blows upon the victim's heart.
But is it glass that cuts or is it jewel?
How grieved the gentle viewers who behold
The rack that from within doth wring a moan,
But do they really think the torturer bold,
Or rather him who suffers pain alone?
Before the fact, would any dare to swear
That he would any suffering gladly face,
Or on his shoulders any weight would bear,
Or under siege quite bravely hold his place?
    Such questions probe the victim's hardy deeds,
    The tyrant is condemned ere he proceeds.

132

Thine eyes I love, and they, as pitying me,
Empower me to hold in cold disdain
Vexation at the fact I'll never be
Full worthy of a worthy lover's pain.
I find within your eyes a very heaven
In which twin orbs have risen from the east
And fix on me their gaze so even,
Before we sink into their warming west.
Ah love, your eyes light up your darling face
And in them I can see your throbbing heart,
As outward signs can show an inward grace
And whole be present in its smallest part.
    The white of day must soon be hid in black,
    But spectra compass colors without lack.

Beshrew that heart that makes my heart to groan
And curse the hand that lifts to threaten me
And all who seek to find me quite alone
That I an easy quarry might then be.
But I would love to be by you thus taken,
And by your sweet talk find myself engrossed
That willingly defense I should forsake.
When you to me through no man's land have crossed
I would forgive with an encouraging word
As lenient judges will open cells to bail
And enemies of all walk past the guard
And make of freedom's city one vast gaol.
    My mind is clouded when I think of thee
    And my heart wants what is not good for me.

"So, now I have confessed that he is thine.
No lover came to work an evil will
Upon me, he is your son as well as mine,
So let suspicion die and lie quite still.
Oh yes, Dame Nature did distribute free
And antickly those traits that in your kind
Are rare. Our son doth far more favor me
Than thee, still shared blood must always bind.
You will indulge me if I sometimes take
From his father what a son may use
And recommend that we for our child's sake
Forego the discipline that changes to abuse.
    So love the boy that so resembles me
    And your dark heart from all suspicions free."

Whoever hath her wish, thou hast thy will,
Which would her wish could be an overplus
Of love for thee and not be wandering still
Mid alien fleshpots, but she does ever thus.
You might of course adopt a mind so spacious
That she could wander ever and still be thine,
Avert your eyes or with a pardon gracious
Forget the rivals who make her eyes so shine.
What you have had is yours in memory still,
However small, it is a permanent store.
Forget who has her wish, have with your will
The memory of what can suffer less no more.
    Or on reflection you may wish to kill
    And thus subject her wish to thy last will.

If thy soul check thee that I come so near,
Thy soul is false so listen to thy will
Which would that your sweet self were ever there
Where we our destiny can best fulfil.
Lovers, denominated thus from love,
Though they be two are longing to be one.
But he his worthiness must also prove
And do what can be done by other none.
True love to strangers will remain untold
The inner never can wholly outer be,
Your hand in mine but in my heart I hold
What only I can know, who lovest thee.

    Deepest run those waters that are still
      And deeds are faint reflections of the will.

137

Thou blind fool, Love, what dost thou to mine eyes
That in her presence I no longer see,
Since seeing deceives me with distorting lies,
As if what seems what is could truly be?
Weighed on the scales of love's blind looks,
Her beauty dazzles, and hunters will ride
And feeding fish will rise to fatal hooks
And slave to oar most cruelly is tied.
So I am blind with love, and if the plot
Is hid I still can tap from place to place,
My reading fingers find what eye cannot
And move across the drama of your face.
      Other senses have so often erred
      Until for truth to touch they were transferred.

When my love swears that she is made of truth,
Could it be logically possible that she lies?
Let greybeards worry the question; impetuous youth
Rightly disdains dialectical subtleties,
Or so at least it was when I was young.
I always spoke with flattery of the best,
Accepted at face value what other tongue
Might say, waiving interest in meanings suppressed.
Talk of the ineffable I thought unjust
And chided the churlish chariness of the old,
A lovely face was one I'd always trust,
Taking for gospel the parables she told.
    The body dangling from that tree is me,
    Who being deceived decided not to be.

O call not me to justify the wrong
That did such damage to your trusting heart,
The truth that came so trippingly to my tongue
Learned falsity in learning love's dark art.
If seeing really were believing, sight
Could not deceive, but ears are deaf to an aside
Which alters 'will' to the subjunctive 'might',
And covertly packs while promising to bide.
This is the truth that every lover knows,
Sooner or late: no worse enemies
Are found than friends who've altered into foes,
But lovers' hands do deepest injuries.
    Would that I in truthful youth were slain
    Than aged and jaded I should give you pain.

140

Be wise as thou art cruel; do not press
The dark advantage of unkind disdain.
The wise are meant to order, so please express
Your will and I'll give pleasure with my pain.
Unloved lovers, all swains that were
Coldly received, disbelieving it was so,
Pressed on, and only when they drew too near
The flame and fatally fell their fate did know.
Love is a madness but O how doubly mad
Am I whose love is not returned by thee.
The absence of the good defines the bad,
Just so, not to be loved is not to be.
    Your unreceptive coldness was belied
    When once you welcomed me with arms so wide.

In faith, I do not love thee with mine eyes
For they are crossed, as you perhaps will note,
And give me doubled objects to despise
And doubled also those on which I dote.
Forget my eyes, with you I am delighted
By other senses, for are not lovers prone
To accept advances whenever they're invited,
At least when they are sure they're quite alone?
Consider this hand which I by lifting can
Move just so until it rests on thee,
It's restless there since I am but a man
Who in touching thee touched too would be.
    The tottering tortoise on the hare will gain
    And pleasure is the remedy for pain.

142

Love is my sin, and thy dear virtue hate
When will you a virtue make of loving
Lest I by your indifference change my state,
Repenting of my love and your reproving?
No devotion through every thick and thin
Remains, nor cheerful birds long ornament
A leafless tree whose sap has drained like time.
O hateful love, but own thy raiment's rents.
Among philosophers and cynics those
Are found who would with argument prove thee
Right in giving hate for love, so grows
A cancer by division, no more to be.
    Dire darling, I cannot hope to hide
    That I would be affirmed and not denied.

Lo as a careful housewife runs to catch
The skulking postman lest he get away
Before with him she can a check dispatch
That might a creditor's cruel hand stay,
But he's already left and she gives chase,
Kimono clad and slippered, running hell bent
After him while at the pane a neighbor's face
Observes pursuer and pursued with discontent.
This is a metaphor of me and thee.
Limping of course, as laggard I behind
The ample disappearing back you turn to me.
I huff and puff and wish that you were kind.
    Limbs lumber at command of will,
    My weary will bids mine be still.

144

Two loves I have, of comfort and despair,
Both thwarted, as it happens, both still
Trumped by love for one so cruelly fair
That I must hope to have her or fall ill.
But there is one who prompts us to do evil,
Mistake the losing for the winning side,
Who once was heaven-high in bliss. That devil
Plunged like feathered comet for his pride,
And now his loss to share that lying fiend
Would in confidential whisper tell
You first to doubt and then betray your friend
And by your treachery plunge him into hell.
    O darling, douse the feeble flame of doubt
    And come inside where you may find me out.

Those lips that Love's own hand did make
Were never made that they might twist in hate
Or wound a gentle heart for mere spite's sake,
Behaving quite against the love of you I state.
Your beauty pristine from its maker come
Did fill the hearts about you with rue sweet.
So joyed that had the trumpet sounded doom
They would have run while laughing out to greet
Apocalypse itself, since you the end
Did mark of all before, as sun the day
Begins, defeating the nocturnal fiend
And by its brightness burns the night away.
 No random dice a gambling maker threw
 But fashioned artfully thy face and you.

Poor soul, the center of my sinful earth
That spins darkly among the stars' array
A spirit incorporeal by dearth
Of lightness sinks like Satan down the gay
Sky to burrow ice-deep in earth and leave
Its frozen self. My capital I spend
To buy you back from selfish sad excess,
Remorselessly causing remorse to end.
A value is known only by its loss,
Prodigals, we view the empty store
Where gold is gone and there is only dross,
Less, then least, then naught remaining more.
    If youth could heed the wisdom had by men
    I would not now be ruing what was then.

My love is as a fever, longing still
For what preceded that so dire disease
That poisons the wells of sentiment and makes me
    ill,
But longing colors pain and makes it please.
What lover can recall a time when love
Had not yet dawned and still its secret kept,
Nor could one think he'd not approve
Its advent, or anything imagine except
This. What folly to think that love could care
For logic, allowing the novice in his unrest
To know or care just what conditions are
Apropos: only by passion is it expressed.
    The colors quite distinct when day is bright
    Merge into black with advent of the night.

148

O me, what eyes hath Love put in my head
That filter out all else except the sight
Of thee. Westward has my lengthened shadow fled,
But light and shade I do not see aright,
So let me with these lover's eyes still dote
Upon thy beauty that fills my vision so
That words will rhyme that once did but denote,
And Yes is wrung from heart intending No.
Those lacking love will take the false for true,
And where we laugh they look for bitter tears.
The sun perhaps distorts their cold-eyed view
And they must miss the truth that love but clears.

    The one who cannot see is counted blind
    So love must unlove blindness find.

Canst thou, O cruel! Say I love thee not
When you with me did frequently partake
Of that so sweet exchange you've now forgot,
When we did live but for the other's sake.
Had you been not my love but just my friend,
And arm in arm had oft embarked upon
The river in the moonlight there to spend
A silent while relieved by tender moan,
Would I or anyone of reason then expect
Your fell forgetfulness? How then despise
Your erstwhile love? Or pretend that each defect
Could come from else than your dishonest eyes?

    Please cease to bother with your mind
    And be, like other wide-eyed windows, blind.

O from what power hast thou this powerful might
That makes the visible world to sway
And obscures for even keenest sight
What otherwise would be as plain as day?
Thus love did mighty Samson make so ill
He could no longer do those mighty deeds,
For there was one possessed of subtle skill
By which the weak the stronger sex exceeds.
Conquered by love, we crave its onslaught more,
And would not for the world embrace its cousin hate.
Indeed we're taught by love to quite abhor
A victory whose victor is not left in conquered state.
     The power that love has lent you over me
     Is just the power that I have over thee.

Love is too young to know what conscience is,
But conscience knows a thing or two of love
And often finds its tenderness amiss,
But how but tenderly could love quite prove
It's true. Coward-making conscience could betray
The lover's move, call fidelity treason,
Until reproved, demoralized, lovers may
Think their cold accuser speaks but reason.
I am no longer young but I love thee
Conscientiously and with the pride
Of knowing that you must eventually be
Standing before the altar at my side.
    The heart must heed whenever love should call,
    Remaining upright, waiting but to fall.

152

In loving thee thou knowst I am forsworn
From loving others, you may hear them swearing
In outer darkness, faces distraught, garments torn,
Convinced your winning of me is past all bearing
Do not think that I begrudge to thee
Exclusive claim on me, make the most
Of what you have while I am sworn to thee.
How long can I to others all be lost?
Saint Paul advises killing foes with kindness,
So I will wear you down with constancy,
So fill your eyes with beauty you'll crave blindness,
As those deprived of sight cry out to see.
    The joker whom you hear is only I,
    Like every lover I do love to lie.

153

Cupid laid by his brand and fell asleep
When a wandering scholar that brand found
And sought to sell it for a price too steep,
He failed and flung it back upon the ground.
Something like that may hap to one in love,
Who with reversals finds he can't endure,
Nor understand those little tests that prove
If Cupid's dart went deep enough to cure.
That aforesaid brand my heart has hotly fired
And sweetest pain so blazes in my breast
I no longer know which is more desired,
The fire or some soft salve, the host or guest.
    Familiar beauty that before us lies
    Becomes visible when love lights up our eyes.

The little Love-god lying once asleep
Received upon his bottom a searing brand.
The culprit thought that thereby he could keep
Love corralled and bound both foot and hand.
Thou fool, Prometheus stole fire,
Which being stolen him no longer warmed.
Just so the rustler's criminal desire
Will end by seeing him alone disarmed.
Love is more surely and securely kept by
One who gives his love away in perpetual
Loving. A paradoxical remedy:
One is most free when one is most in thrall.
    Of course if one is given tests to prove
    Himself, the tester is not moved by love.